Emoji ABCs

Express Yourself – Discover communication through emotions

Content By Judine Bishop, PhD

Copyright © 2024 by Judine Bishop, PhD
Making My Ancestors Proud

All rights reserved
Published by United Black Writers Association, Inc.

No part of this book may be reproduced or transmitted in any form or by any means, electronic or mechanical, including photocopying, recording, or by any information storage and retrieval system without the publisher's or contributors' written permission.

Teaching communication through emojis.
Both young and old will enjoy it.
Designed with you in mind ... Judine Bishop, PhD

Each emoji has a question to serve as a guide for self-reflection or as a prompt in discussions about emotional expression.

For more information, contact:
By Any Ink Necessary
400 East Pratt Street, 8th Floor
Baltimore, MD 21202

https://bit.ly/m/byanyinknecessary

Affectionate

How do you usually express happiness when you care about someone?

Baffled

How do you let someone know you're confused or unsure about something?

Crushed

How do you express disappointment without being harsh?

Daunted

How do you express your emotions when you feel left out or excluded?

Expressionless

How do you communicate when you're feeling bored?

Frowning

When you feel sad, how do you prefer to let others know?

Grimacing

What are your ways of communicating frustration in a difficult situation?

Hoodwinked

What's your approach to expressing playful trickery?

Intimidated

When you're feeling afraid, how do you convey that to others?

Joyful

What's your go-to method for expressing gratitude?

Kind

What's your approach to expressing a good mood to others?

Lively

How do you communicate when you're feeling optimistic?

Mischievous

When would you playfully cause trouble?

Nervous

How do you let others know what you're experiencing when you feel anxious?

Overwhelmed

How do you communicate when you have too much to do?

Preoccupied

How do you let others know you are busy? How will you let them know when you have the time?

Quizzical

How do you gently express that you do not understand?

Rage

How should you express anger toward people who are in charge?

Sullen

How do you express your feelings of nostalgia or longing?

Thinking

How do you express your feelings of nostalgia or longing?

Unamused

What's your way of showing that you're stressed?

Vicious

How could you stop feelings of being cruel or violent?

Whisper

When are times you would use a quiet voice?

Xanadu

How do you show that you're at peace or tranquil?

Yucky

How do you let someone know you're not feeling good, physically or emotionally?

Zany

How do you share when you are feeling whimsically comical?

JUDINE BISHOP, PhD
Author/Instructor/Motivational Coach

PROFILE
Judine has empowered stories and elevated writers for the past 10 years by offering workshops, conferences, interviews, and book publishing. She collaborates with authors and other businesses by working closely with clients to identify areas for improvement and develop strategies to enhance productivity.

CONTACT
PHONE: (301) 742-8005

ADDRESS: 400 East Pratt Street
Floor, Baltimore, MD 21202

EMAIL: blackwriters@gmail.com

Judine Bishop was a divorced Mother of three, with the oldest about to graduate high school. She suggested her daughter Rebecca publish some of her poetry to qualify for college scholarships. After publishing "No Sweat: Poems of an American Youth," Rebecca accepted a $10K per year scholarship from Trinity University. With this success, Judine transcribed letters written in pig Latin and backward text to publish her memoir, "Clear Skinned."

Judine initiated a writer's association in Prince George's County and collaborated with 50+ writers or authors to present topics about writing or publishing for monthly meetings at a local bookstore to promote both writers and books. She also contracted with The Mall at Prince George for three annual Afrocentric Book Expos, where 90+ authors had the opportunity to sell their books. The Black Quill is a commemorative journal of these activities.

When independent and corporate bookstores began closing, Judine interviewed 30+ business owners about the essentials of writing on the By Any Ink Necessary Facebook live show. Judine transcribed seven interviews for the book "Writing is Essential: Use The Skills You've Got to Get the Job Done."

After receiving a PhD in Education – Instructional Design and Technology, Judine started an editing and publishing consulting business called By Any Ink Necessary with the online course Write to Publish.

WEBSITE: https://bit.ly/m/byanyinknecessary

The history of emojis is a fascinating journey through technology, culture, and communication. Here's a brief overview:

Origins and Early Developments - Late 1990s: Early Concepts

Shigetaka Kurita: In 1999, Shigetaka Kurita, a Japanese designer, first developed the concept of emojis. Kurita worked for NTT DoCoMo, a Japanese mobile communications company. He created a set of 176 simple, pixelated icons to help users convey emotions and information quickly on their phones. These icons included smiley faces, weather symbols, and other everyday items.

Global Expansion - 2007: Unicode Standardization

The Unicode Consortium, responsible for maintaining text standards across different platforms, began incorporating emojis into its Unicode standard. This move was crucial for ensuring emojis could be used across various devices and operating systems.

Cultural Impact and Evolution - 2014: Unicode Emoji Expansion

The Unicode Consortium expanded the range of emojis to include more diverse and representative symbols, including a wider array of facial expressions, activities, and symbols reflecting global culture.

Emojis in Communication

Emojis have become integral to digital communication, influencing text messaging, social media, marketing, and even art. They convey emotions, reactions, and nuanced meanings in ways that text alone sometimes cannot.

The development of emojis reflects a broader trend towards more visual and expressive forms of digital communication, highlighting how technology can shape and enhance our interactions.

History generated by ChatGPT. https://chatgpt.com/

Emoji images from htttps://Pixabay.com

www.ingramcontent.com/pod-product-compliance
Lightning Source LLC
Chambersburg PA
CBHW042010150426
43195CB00002B/86